Take Heart, O Ye of Little Faith

By

Annette G. Cooper

ISBN: 0-7596-7400-0 (ebook)
ISBN: 0-7596-7401-9 (Paperback)

This book is printed on acid free paper.

1stBooks - rev. 10/9/02

DEDICATION

I dedicate this book to my Lord and Savior, Jesus Christ, who inspired me to write this book. The spirit of our Lord and Savior said, "Write a book." I repeated the statement, "Write a book?" "Yes", he said, and the spirit of the Lord reminded me of a dream. The comforter, which is the Holy Spirit whom the Father will send in my name, he will teach you all things and bring to your remembrance whatsoever I have said unto you.

I also dedicate this book to my children, Felicia, Kersichia, Charmell, and Antonio.

PREFACE: Experiencing Faith In God

Thinking about what the spirit of the Lord said brought a thought to my mind. Am I experiencing faith in God or am I bringing it to mind and not releasing it to God? Well, I asked God how to experience faith in him. First, let us find out what experiencing mean. Experiencing means encountering or undergoing things as they occur in the course of time. Second, what is faith? **Hebrews 11:1,** "Now faith is the substance of things hoped for, the evidence of things not seen." It is impossible to please the Lord without faith. For he is a rewarder of them that diligently seek him. Third, we put our trust in God, he is faithful. **II Peter 3:9,** "The Lord is not slack concerning his promise as some count slackness, but is long suffering toward us."

INTRODUCTION

To have faith in God gives us the assurance from God Almighty to take one day at a time to know that God will supply our every need; they will be met through him. Whatever it is, believe in God, for he will not fail you. Whatever problems you have, trust and believe in God. By faith my life is in control; I put my trust in him. To put your trust in anything else but God will fail. Nothing will give you security; not your job or eternal life in your friends. Only God can give you security. There is eternal life in Jesus. This is a promise. **I Thessalonians 4:16, 18**.

KEEP YOUR FOCUS

WHAT IS FAITH?

Faith is trusting in God, believing that he loves us and knows what is best for our good. Instead of our own, it leads us to choose his way. In place of our ignorance, it accepts his wisdom. In place of our weakness, his strength. In place of our sinfulness, his righteous faith is the gift of God, but the power to exercise it is ours. Faith is the hand by which the soul takes hold upon the Divine offers of grace and mercy. Exercising faith is more difficult when circumstances are good, in times of prosperity, when there seems to be less call for faith, which often diminishes. How then can and does faith grow?

Our faith is based upon what the Scriptures have declared, that "Jesus died and rose from the dead and ascended into heaven." **Romans 10:9,** "That if thou shalt confess with thy mouth the Lord Jesus, and shalt believe in thine heart that God hath raised him from the dead, thou shalt be saved."

BY FAITH IN GOD

Psalms 91:1&2, "He who dwells in the shelter of the most high will rest in the shadow of the Almight. I will say of the Lord, he is my refuge and my fortress, my God, in him will I trust." My husband tied me to the bed and said he was going to cut my throat out. Before he came home, the Lord told me to anoint the bed from head to toes. By faith, I obeyed Jesus and my life was spared that night. You see, I know the Lord, by faith what he can do. **Psalms 91:3&4,**

"Surely he will save you from the fowler's prey and from the deadly pestilence. He will cover you with his feathers and under his wings you will find refuge; his faithfulness will be your shield and comfort."

Romans 4:17, "As it is written, I have made thee father of many nations, before him whom he believed, even God, who quickeneth the dead, and calleth those things which be not as though they were." Exercising the God kind of faith—I believe it therefore I will receive it.

Having faith in God will allow you to wait on the Lord. I wanted to attend a church conference that was coming up. I did not have the money, but I was speaking like I knew God would supply the money. I prayed the prayer of faith, "Lord, I do not want to borrow the money." I wanted God to supply my needs

according to his purpose. I was talking to another Christian about how I believed God would provide the money. Glory be to God, he used that sister to buy my ticket. I was speaking and releasing my faith in my Lord Jesus. Faith will go in any direction you release it in. Without faith it is impossible to please God. Isn't it great to know what pleases God?

Faith, without a shadow of doubt, is the key to pleasing the Lord. "Without faith it is impossible to please him". An individual uses the expression, "You have good luck". I haven't come across anyone who said, "You have faith in God". I plant my seed of faith daily, depending totally on the Lord, Jesus Christ, to supply my needs. I take one day at a time. Lord, I am depending on you to supply my needs and direct my path. Glory to God, who gives us the victory. I asked

the Lord, "Who do I talk to?" and "Lord, whatever you want me to do, I am here".

I know someone might be saying, "Lord I believed that you were going to save my children, but it seems like they are getting worst". Stand on the word of God. If he said he will do it, praise be to God. God is not a man who would lie.

O, ye of little faith. If you are seeking wisdom, by faith you can have it. He says, "If any of you lack wisdom, let him ask God who gives to all liberally and without reproach, and it will be given to him." But let him ask in faith without doubting." We can help others when they ask how much we trust and depend on God. On the job, walk in faith, on campus, exercise your faith and always remember "Faith without works is dead". Individuals will notice the difference in you, and some will come and question you about why you

don't worry about this and that. Why should we worry? God has it all under control. "Today is the day that the Lord has made. I will rejoice and be glad in it." "Have faith in God", **Mark 11:22**. Worry is the lack of trust in God.

God has given us his word. Faith is acting on the word. I know God's word is true. I know that God promised me certain things I should have. When we pray in faith, we have attained it. The word of God says I have it now even though I cannot see it. Faith says I have it. Faith says I have it now because God promised it. **Hebrews 11:1**, "Now faith is the substance of things hoped for and the evidence of things not seen."

TOUCH JESUS

Where is your faith? We need to examine ourselves to see if we are in the faith.

Sometimes our faith is going to be tested. Abraham's faith was tried. God told Abraham to take his son, his only son. He obeyed and God provided the sacrifice. Abraham knew that God said he was going to bless him with a son who would be the son of promise. Isaac was born to Abraham and Sarah as a result of a covenant promise. Abraham reverenced God and his confidence was in God's faithfulness to keep his covenant promise. Abraham knew and had the assurance that God would raise Isaac up from the dead **(Hebrews 11:19)**.

Daniel and his friends refused to bow down and worship the image that was made by the king. Because of this Shadrach, Meshach, and Abednego were put in the fiery furnace. "Our God whom we serve is able to deliver us from your hands, O king. But if not, let it be known to you, O king, that we do not serve your gods, nor will we worship the golden image which you have set up." **(Daniel 3:17, 18)**. This is how we need to be when it comes to serving our God, trusting him that if he delivers us or not, he is able.

RELEASE IT TO JESUS

Release, as Webster's defines it, means "to set free". **John 8:32,** says "And ye shall know the truth, and the truth shall make you free". Release everything to Jesus because he cares for you and me. **I Peter 5:7**, "Cast all your cares upon him, for he careth much for you." Jesus wants to set us free in the way we look at our situation. My prayer request for my son was, "Lord, make a miracle in my son's life," and God is doing just that all because I released him the Lord believing that God is not slack concerning his promise. **Psalms 37:4**, "Delight thyself also in the Lord; and he shall give thee the desires of thine heart." We need to know how to use our faith. God wants us to come to his throne boldly. **Hebrews 4:16**, "Let us therefore come bodly unto the throne of grace, that we may obtain mercy, and find grace to help in time of need."

When I started writing this book, the Lord spoke to me concerning Abraham taking a journey in faith. Abraham was a man of faith and also received great blessings from the Lord. The Lord reminded me about **Deuteronomy 28**. "Do all which I command thee this day, that the Lord thy God will set thee on high above all nations of the earth." Have faith in God. "Blessed shall thou be in the city." I do not care where you are, God is able to bless you. "Blessed shall thou be in the field." God will bless when you go to the store for groceries, believing that my God's work is true. "Blessed shall be the fruit of your body," not only with children, but youth, strength with health of body. "Blessed coming in, blessed going out." Why can't we rest in knowing that God has it all in control? All we need is faith in God.

"Release it to the Lord," **I Peter 5:7**, believing that God is able to supply, **Phillipians 4:19**. Watch and pray because God is not slack concerning his promise. "Keep your mind on him, because he will keep you in peace, **Isaiah 26:3**. Putting your trust in him, **Proverbs 28:26**. We must worship him in spirit and trust. Let us also remember our faith works with love; our confession of his lordship in our lives is to be consistent daily with deep gratitude because we walk by faith and not by sight. By faith we accept the work of God as to who Jesus is and why he came into the world. Through faith, our confession is steadfast. Only faith can make you look beyond the present situation.

On the day I was to have foot surgery, the enemy said, "They are going to give you too much anesthesia." I said, "If they do, I will be with Jesus."

That is how much faith I have in my Lord and Savior Jesus Christ. I said, "Lord, it is just you and me." He said "Look at those chair." In the room, there were about a dozen chairs. He said, "There are angel in every one of them." Listen to Jesus. Do you know what I did? I believed him. Glory, glory to God who gives us the victory. I love it when the spirit of the Lord speaks. What happens when we release? Let me rephrase that. What happens when we think we have released our faith in the Lord? As time goes on and you have not received, do you give up? Do you start murmuring? You have to have faith in God. Why are you so fearful, O, ye of little faith? Yes, God can move your mountain right now.

James 1:6, "But let him asking faith nothing wavering. For he that wavereth is live a wave of the sea driven with the wind and tossed." A double

minded man is unstable in all his ways. Put your trust in God and wait on him to bring things to pass. We want God to move at our convenience. It does not work that way. A little bit of faith can remove a mountain, but with it there is no doubt. What is my motive when I believe God will move that mountain in my life? Is it to show how great a faith I have or what? Be careful, to God be the glory, not to you or me, but God Almighty. God, you delivered the children of Israel.

"By faith in God, you will not fear the terrors of night, nor the arrow that flies by day, nor the pestilence that stalks in the darkness, nor the plaque that destroys at midday, **Psalms 91:5&6**. A demon was living by me. I mean a lady who had a demon in her was plotting to kill me. I did not know she had just gotten out of the mental institution. I had become friends

with her and took her to church a couple of times. She had delusions and possessing by a demon to get rid of me. She had knives and matches hidden in the hall on my floor. She took the bulbs in the upstairs hall so that when I came in from church she could attack me, but God knew her thought. The Lord changed my arrival time one night and I came in early, so the plot did not work. By faith, prayer was set up and own those stairs and the Lord saw to it that the lady moved the next day. Not two later days later, but he next day she was gone. So you see what faith in my lord and Savior can do. **Psalms 91:9&10**, "If you make the Most High your dwelling, even the land who is my refuge, then no harm will befall you, no disaster will come near your tent"

Faith is shown when we speak those things that are not as though they exist. I received jobs this way. There was a job I wanted in a hospital. I was told the hospital was not hiring, but the Lord said they were. Through faith in my Lord, I was hired. One year my car came by faith. I prayed "Lord, I need another car. I don't see any way." I asked God in prayer, believing he would supply the car. I did not give up or lose faith in my Lord and he did as I had prayed. I received my car; the Lord told me what color it was and everything. By faith I have purchased items because I knew what I wanted and I walked by faith. Don't lose hope in God, because he will fulfill, by faith, that which we believe, that which we will see through Jesus. By faith in what we belive in, our heart shall confess with our mouth, Lord Jesus, believe in your heart that God has raised him from the dead and you shall be saved because God

said it. Faith is in speaking and hearing God's word. In Genesis 1, God said, "Let there be", and it was through him speaking it.

Because of your faith, the devil is going to come against you, no matter how much you trust God. Our faith in God is the key to receiving when you believe that God loves you and wants to give you what you need. Whatever your needs are, God has it. Salvation, health, finances, every good thing we desire with your faith in God, no matter how small, God can do the impossible.

The spirit of the Lord spoke to me in a dream saying, "O, ye of little faith." I was looking for a miracle and I did not see any way. Notice my statement, "I was looking for a miracle and I did not see any way." I was lacking confidence and faith in Jesus. My trust was in "I". Jesus used this statement

in various situations as a tender rebuke or corrective chiding. **Matthew 8:24-26,** "And, behold, there arose a great tempest in the sea, in so much that the ship was covered with the waves; but he (Jesus) was asleep. And his disciples came to him, and awoke him, saying, Lord, save us: we perish. And he said unto them, Why are ye fearful, O YE OF LITTLE FAITH?" Now it is evident where I got the title. We do not need to question God. Say, all right God, at your command, not my will but your will be done. O, ye of little faith. When God tell us to do something, the way is already made. We need to flow with the spirit, doubting nothing. Oh, praise be to God. God has it all under control. Right now, stop and ask God to meet that need in your life. God's word says that he would supply all your needs according to his riches in glory **(Philippians 4:19).**

GOD CAN

BY FAITH

When I started working where I am currently employed, I wanted to work five days a week; Monday through Friday, but I was unable to get that schedule. I prayed about it and kept speaking on it. I was at work one night and had just gotten through asking once more for God to give me Monday through Friday, as had others who were praying for me by faith. Within ten minutes the phone rang. It was my supervisor. She said, "Annette, I want to know would you like to work 3 to 11 Monday through Friday?" I told my supervisor yes. I informed her that I had been praying for this. She said, "You got it, but there is one thing I want you to do and that is train the new staff person." I said, "No problem." God is so good. His word says in Isaiah 65:24, "And it shall come to pass, that before they call, I will answer; and while they are yet

speaking I will hear." By faith in God, we can move a mountain.

PROTECTION

"By faith the Lord will order your steps," **Psalms 37:23**. One night the Lord ordered my steps. He showed me what to do by faith and by my doing it by faith in the Lord, my life was spared to be here this day.

Even today my health, and the degree to which I may age, is in God's hands. By faith in him, he renews me day by day. My Lord and Savior Jesus reminds me how much he loves me, and through my faith in him, he renews my youth. He cherishes me and he also shows me how much he loves me. In his word he says how he will beautify the meek. **Psalms 103:4 & 5**, "Who redeemeth thy life from destruction; who

crowneth thee with living kindness and tender mercies; who satisfieth thy mouth with good things so that thy youth is renewed like the eagles."

By faith, he is my protector, my provider, my healer, and my deliverer. Release the situation to him, and Jesus will keep his word in due season. We should not be weary or doubtful over God meeting our needs. We should claim them by faith since God promises them to us. We have an unlimited supply that can be met through God. There is nothing impossible for him; we need to be faithful to him and leave the results to him.

NEEDS MET IN THIS DAY AND TIME

SUPPLIER

I relocated to New York City with only enough money for cab fare and no place to stay. The Lord told me to got there, so I knew without a doubt that he would supply what I needed: a place to stay, a job, and clothes. An evangelist gave me a place to stay and she also helped me locate an aunt I knew who lived there. My aunt was working in a hospital and I went to see if she could help me get a job there as well. She told me, "No", because they were closing down the facility. It was true about the closing, but God kept it open long enough to get me hired and transferred. Then the facility was closed. That's just like my God. He said so many times that he would supply my needs, and I need to continue to trust and believe in him.

I think back to how I had so much faith in my job that I knew my paycheck would be there when it was all the time. Sometime I was so disappointed, but not with my Lord and Savior. If he said he would do it, then he would. I have learned to put my trust in Jesus and not man. **Psalms 1:3,** "And he shall be like a tree planted by the rivers of water, that brings forth his fruit in his season; his leaf also shall not wither, and whatsoever he doeth shall prosper." **Matthew 6:30,** "Now, if God so clothes the grass of the field, which today is and tomorrow is thrown into the oven, will he not much more clothe you, O ye of little faith; there do not worry." Let us move that mountain out of our lives. **Matthew 17:20,** Jesus said, "If you have faith as a mustard seed, you will say to this mountain, move from here to there; and it will move and nothing will be impossible for you." Why not try it? It works.

GODS RESOURCES ARE UNLIMITED

The divine economy has no shortage. God's supply always equals our needs. God does not want any of his people to have any lack. You can apply your faith to see your daily needs met. You sow the mustard seed, the smallness of your faith, into an action. Believe God and he will supply. Hallelujah.

God is willing to heal, but at the same time, one cannot intentionally be living in violation of God's will. Even if our faith in his sovereign purpose does not bring healing, nevertheless, in all things let us praise him for his faithfulness and compassion. **Matthew 8:16,** says to always realize that Jesus is willing to heal. **Mark 5:24 & 34.** This is clearly seen in this passage.

Mark 11:24, "Therefore, I say to you, whatsoever things you ask when you pray believe that you receive them and you will have them." From Jesus we receive the direct and practical instruction concerning exercising our faith of the almighty. One is the sources and grounds of our faith and being. Jesus words "whatsoever things" should be applied to every aspect of our lives. Our faith must be in God that we believe not doubting in our hearts. Our faith in God is the key to receiving. When you believe that God loves you and wants to give you your needs, then your believing creates faith in your heart. With faith believe and receive salvation, health, wealth, and goods things we desire. Faith in God no matter how small can do the impossible. All things are possible with God.

Nothing matters when you pray the prayer of faith, but believe God is going to do it. Keep repeating what the word of God has to say about the matter. I know there is someone who is reading this book and saying, "But, Lord." Throw that word right out of your mind. Release it to Jesus and go your way. He is working it out. I will share this with the Lord. I just want to thank you, Lord, for being so good. I remember this like it was yesterday. The kids and I moved to South Carolina with an aunt who did not believe in sharing at all. We did not have anything to eat at that time. My aunt had a friend who lived down the street where we lived; therefore I took the family there. My children and I sat down at that table where we only had a few pieces of bread and some jelly to eat. The children looked at me, and I said with tears in my eyes and said, "Lord, we thank you because I know tomorrow you

will bless us with food." People, God is real. The next day God blessed us with so much food I was pressed to fill the freezer with it. I thank God for the food. God knew my heart. I prayed the prayer of faith. I did not murmur nor complain. I learned to be content in whatever condition I have been in (Philippians **4:11**). I know without a doubt in my heart that God will provide for us. I am really blessed to have the chance to write this book. Take Heart, O Ye of Little Faith, but oh, to have trust in Jesus is so powerful. Do not worry about others who seems t have more than the eye can bear. Seek Jesus. He will bring sunshine into your life. Let us stop and thank God for what he is doing right now. Thank you, God, for Jesus.

While you are believing in God for everything, he wants us to thank him. Also, he wants us to take time out and worship him. Next, he wants us to love him. No greater love have I received than from my Lord and Savior, who laid down his life for me. God so love the world that he gave us his only begotten son. Let's have peace. He said in his word, "I will keep you in perfect peace whose mind is stayed on me." Let's praise God for his goodness. **Psalms 31:19,** "How great is they goodness."

I am giving thanks to my Lord and Savior, Jesus Christ for two dear sisters in the Lord, who by faith stepped in to help me get my manuscript typed. Rhonda Dean and Neeta Williams. I prayed, "Lord, I need help." One thing about it, he tells you to do something and the way is already made. All we need to do is have faith in him. Thanks to the Lord for

touching these to precious hearts. **Hebrews 11:6,** "But without faith it is impossible to please him; for he that cometh to God must believe that he is, and that he is the rewarder of them that diligently seek him." Have you thought about what the word of God is saying. It is impossible to please God without faith.

Believing God for the possible. I wrote a check, believing God would supply the money to cover it. (Let me be clear, I do not write checks to try God, this was a need.) The next day, after work, I checked my mail only to find a check from my health insurance company. God is faithful. I knew he would provide because he does it all the time. The check was three months due. God knew when I would need the money. He's an on time God. The spirit of the Lord let me know that I needed to take the limit off him and to not

worry about tomorrow. Tomorrow will take care of itself. God has it all under control.

We must hold on to our faith in our Lord and Savior, Jesus Christ. The nations around us are crumbling; crime and confusion are everywhere. But through it all, we have assurance in God. Our faith in the coming king is the only hope we have. Do not give up because we walk by faith and not by sight. As Jesus said, "Fear not, for we have the promise that we all shall not sleep." For the Lord himself descend from heaven with a shout with the trumpet call of god; and the dead in Christ shall rise first; then we who are alive shall be caught up together with them in the clouds to meet the Lord in the air. We shall forever be with the Lord. The only way we can look at the unseen is by faith.

NEEDS

O, ye of little faith, all your needs can be met in Jesus Christ. Our father knows our needs. **Matthew 6:8,** "For your father knows what things ye have need of before you ask him." I could remember a time when I would depend on my children when I needed something. Oh, but my children failed to help me with my needs. Then I would say to myself, I know my friend will help me meet my needs. But they failed too. Deep down inside, I would hear the voice of God saying that he would supply All, not one, two or three, but all my needs according to his riches in glory.

I remember a while back when my car would not start, I went dead. I was in the parking lot and I got in the car and tried to start it, but it would not start. I got out and put up the hood, went to the trunk, and got the jumper cables. I looked around to see if some

gentlemen would help me, but no one did. I said, "Lord, it just you and me." I had faith in God to believe that he would start his car. Glory be to God, he did. The Holy Spirit said, "Put the cables on the battery, spread the other end of the cables on the cement, now start the car." By faith in my Lord and Savior, Jesus Christ, my car started. God said he would supply all my needs. **Philippians 4:19,** "But my God shall supply all your nees according to his riches in glory by Christ Jesus."

Sometime ago, before I came to the reality that God would supply my needs, I tried to fulfill them on my own strength, failing every time. Thanks to God the for the victory over the devil and the way I was thinking. **Psalms 23:1.** "Lord is my shepherd, I shall not want." This Lord is so good. His word is true. Oh, fear the Lord, ye his saints, for there is no want to them that fear him, the reverence fear. The young lions do lack, and suffer hunger; but hey that seek the Lord shall not want any good thing. Believe that God will do it.

TRUST GOD

HEALER

I know my Savior as a healer. An accident happened to my son that involved him falling down seven or more stairs. When I pick him up, his mouth was filled with blood. Just at that instant, I called on my lord and Savior, Jesus Christ, to heal my son's mouth. The blood dried up and the Lord brought to my remembrance, **Exodus 14:16,** "But lift thou up thy God, and stretch out thine hand over the sea, and divide it. And the children of Israel shall go on dry ground through the midst of the sea." The verse was perfect. "And stretch out thine hand over the sea, and divide it and they went across on dry land." Yes, God dried his mouth out; no blood in sight by faith in God. He said, "Stretch your hand over his mouth and say Jesus.' I did just that. Hallelujah for Jesus.

Once more knowing Jesus as a healer, having faith in my Lord and Savior. I was home one night alone and do not remember how I fell over my broom, but I do recall when I fell, my right knee bone cam completely out of place. I was on the floor in great pain. I laid there then I called on the name of Jesus. He immediately put the bone back in place. The Lord performed surgery on my knee. He is a good God.

When all else fails, trust God. He hears they cry of his saints. I have had many challenges sense I have been writing this book. All to do with my faith in God. I had been having trouble with my car, and I did not see any money in sight. My savings was depleted, and nothing to spare in my checking. I was in a fix. I drove to work or a week holding up traffic, praying all the time to the Lord, "Why am I going through this again?" I prayed one night and I couldn't come up with anything. I said "Lord, give the angels charge over me, because I will be driving to work." I drove my car to work not knowing what was going to happen on the way there. I got there slowly, but I got there. I am still saying, "Lord, I do not see anyway I can get my car fix." I took it to the shop and asked the mechanic how much it would cost to have a tune up. This is what the spirit of the Lord told me the car

needed through reading an article in a book. The man told me how much it would cost. I still did not have the money. I told him "Thank you", and left. The spirit spoke to me and said, "You need your car, to go to work." So I went back to the shop and told the man to go ahead and fix it. I left my car and the Lord told me whom to call. I did just what the spirit said, and got the money to have my car fixed. Glory, Glory, Glory, my God is good. I released the problem to the Lord. God knows what to do and who will help you in time of need.

TAKE A JOURNEY OF FAITH

Let us take a journey of faith. Moses was born into the House of Levi. Chosen by God to deliver his people. The people believed when they heard that the Lord had visited the children of Israel and that he had looked upon their afflictions, they bowed their heads and worshipped. Be still as God work. You will see his deliverance in this day and time. God can deliver you from the hand of the enemy. Talk to him, tell him your problems and he will work them out; even when there seems to be no way. "The just shall live my faith." Believe in God no matter how things look. He did it for Moses and the children of Israel. He will do it for you.

As children of God, we must take a journey of faith. Let us be like Abraham who went out not knowing where he was going. By faith he dwelt in the land of promise, as in a foreign country, for he waited for the city, which has foundations whose builder and maker is God **(Hebrews 11:8-10)**. We can demonstrate faith by being obedient to God. To please him for he who comes to God must first believe that he is and that he is a rewarder of those who diligently seek him.

NAAMAN'S LEPROSY HEALED

Naaman could have let pride stop him from receiving his healing, but he did not. The man of God told him to dip in the Jordan River. Naaman did not want to do it because of hidden pride. This hidden pride could have prevented Naaman from receiving his healing. God has a way to bring us out. Through obedience and submission, open he way to health. Healing often awaits obedient action.

Another examples, Jesus healed the ten lepers. One obeyed God by showing himself tot he priests **(Luke 17:14).** Some people give up when they don't see it when they want it or how they want it done. They want immediate healing rather than to seek God for a faith-building step of submission. We have so many examples to go follow and put our faith in the Lord, Jesus Christ.

BIOGRAPHY

Annette Gilbert was born in Savannah, Georgia to the late Sam and Martha Gilbert. She grew up there, went to school, and later married. She is the mother of four children. Annette received and accepted the Lord, Jesus Christ in her life in February 1976. Most of her time is spent serving others.

Author Annette G. Cooper brings to her reader's joy-filled news. *Take Heart, O Ye of Little Faith* contains assurance from her own life experience that to have faith is to have victory.

Repeatedly, during times of trial and testing, the author's declaration of faith brought her through to the fulfillment of her needs, whether for housing, employment, or financial aid. Through faith, her injured son was healed and her own life was spared from the danger of domestic violence. Having read widely in the Scriptures, she has been inspired to think deeply about how to apply their message to daily life. By quoting various passages, the author enlarges our understanding of the Bible. Faith, she tells us, allows us to wait upon the Lord.

A book that demonstrates how we can attain true freedom by releasing our cares to Jesus.

ANNETTE G. COOPER's life exemplifies her writings. She first accepted Jesus into her life in 1976, and since then she has demonstrated the power of faith by devoting most of her time to helping others. She was born and raised in Savannah, Georgia, attending the public schools there. Later she made her home in New York City. She is divorced and the mother of four children.

www.ingramcontent.com/pod-product-compliance
Ingram Content Group UK Ltd.
Pitfield, Milton Keynes, MK11 3LW, UK
UKHW041821200726
13854UKWH00001BA/260

9 780759 674011